FOCUS ON CURRENT EVENTS

VOTING AND ELECTIONS

by Sue Bradford Edwards

Focus Readers
VOYAGER

www.focusreaders.com

Copyright © 2024 by Focus Readers®, Lake Elmo, MN 55042. All rights reserved. No part of this book may be reproduced or utilized in any form or by any means without written permission from the publisher.

Focus Readers is distributed by North Star Editions:
sales@northstareditions.com | 888-417-0195

Produced for Focus Readers by Red Line Editorial.

Content Consultant: David Barker, PhD, Professor of Government, American University

Photographs ©: iStockphoto, cover, 1, 16–17, 30–31; Shutterstock Images, 4–5, 6, 8–9, 11, 21, 22–23, 32, 35, 39, 40, 42–43, 44; Bill Hudson/AP Images, 12; Tracy Sugarman/Jackson State University/HBCUs/Getty Images, 15; Red Line Editorial, 19, 25; Kevin Dietsch/UPI/Alamy, 27; Gerry Broome/AP Images, 29; Paula Bronstein/AP Images, 36–37

Library of Congress Cataloging-in-Publication Data
Names: Edwards, Sue Bradford, author.
Title: Voting and elections / by Sue Bradford Edwards.
Description: Lake Elmo, MN : Focus Readers, 2024. | Series: Focus on current events | Includes index. | Audience: Grades 4-6
Identifiers: LCCN 2023005623 (print) | LCCN 2023005624 (ebook) | ISBN 9781637396452 (hardcover) | ISBN 9781637397022 (paperback) | ISBN 9781637398098 (pdf) | ISBN 9781637397596 (ebook)
Subjects: LCSH: Voting--United States--Juvenile literature. | Elections--United States--Juvenile literature.
Classification: LCC JK1978 .E28 2024 (print) | LCC JK1978 (ebook) | DDC 324.60973--dc23/eng/20230223
LC record available at https://lccn.loc.gov/2023005623
LC ebook record available at https://lccn.loc.gov/2023005624

Printed in the United States of America
Mankato, MN
082023

ABOUT THE AUTHOR

Sue Bradford Edwards is a Missouri nonfiction author. She writes about current events, social science, science, and history. She has written more than 30 titles for young readers including *What Are Learning Disorders?*, *Become a Construction Equipment Operator*, *Being Black in America*, and *Robotics in Health Care*. Shortly after writing this book, she voted in a midterm election.

TABLE OF CONTENTS

CHAPTER 1
2020 Presidential Election 5

CHAPTER 2
History of Voting Rights 9

CASE STUDY
SNCC 14

CHAPTER 3
How US Elections Work 17

CHAPTER 4
Gerrymandering 23

CASE STUDY
Rucho v. Common Cause 28

CHAPTER 5
Restricting Voting 31

CHAPTER 6
Expanding Voting 37

CHAPTER 7
Voter Turnout 43

Focus on Voting and Elections • 46
Glossary • 47
To Learn More • 48
Index • 48

CHAPTER 1

2020 PRESIDENTIAL ELECTION

In 2020, the United States held an election. President Donald Trump was the Republican candidate. He ran against Joe Biden, a Democrat. Election Day was November 3. In past elections, most people voted in person at polling places. But the 2020 election took place during the COVID-19 **pandemic**. To avoid spreading the virus, people were encouraged to avoid crowds. Many people voted early. Most states had several

Most states offer at least one way for people to cast votes before Election Day.

▲ In 2020, 43 percent of voters mailed in their ballots. Another 26 percent used in-person early voting.

ways to do this. Some voters used mail-in ballots. Others went to places that had early voting.

Ballots from early voting are counted on Election Day. But mail-in ballots may arrive later. On the night of November 3, Trump led in several states. However, he lost this lead as mail-in ballots were counted in Pennsylvania and Michigan. When all ballots were counted, Biden was the winner.

Trump and some of his supporters disputed the results. They claimed Biden won through **fraud**. In voter fraud, people may add votes to one side's count. Or they may prevent some votes from being counted. Trump said both things happened in 2020. He claimed votes were cast after the polls closed and mail-in ballots were counted incorrectly.

The US Justice Department investigated these claims. Officials looked for fake or uncounted ballots. They checked that votes had been recorded correctly. They found no signs of widespread fraud.

Reporters also investigated. They, too, found that Trump's claims were false. Yet in 2022, polls found that nearly 70 percent of Republican voters still believed there was fraud. Elections remained a controversial topic.

CHAPTER 2

HISTORY OF VOTING RIGHTS

Voting gives people a say in how their country operates. When the US Constitution took effect in 1789, it allowed each state to decide who could vote. At first, most states permitted only white male landowners to vote. These men had to be at least 21 years old. Some states had religious tests, too. The tests kept Catholic and Jewish people from voting.

The US Constitution lays out the basic laws of the United States, as well as the rights its citizens have.

Over time, these limits changed. By the 1850s, most white men could vote. They no longer had to own land. Other key changes happened after the US Civil War (1861–1865). In 1865, for example, the Thirteenth **Amendment** ended slavery. In 1868, the Fourteenth Amendment gave Black Americans the same rights as other US citizens. And in 1870, the Fifteenth Amendment gave Black men the right to vote. It also said states couldn't make laws that kept people from voting because of their race.

However, many Southern states passed laws that limited voting rights in other ways. Some laws required that voters own property or be able to read. Other laws made voters pay a poll tax. People who couldn't pay this fee could not vote. These rules and tests were often ignored for white voters. But they kept many Black men from voting.

▲ Women who called for the right to vote were known as suffragettes. They organized many protests.

Meanwhile, other groups worked to gain the right to vote. In 1920, the Nineteenth Amendment gave this right to women. But people of color still faced barriers. In 1924, a new law recognized **Indigenous** people as US citizens. Until then, they hadn't been able to register to vote. In 1943, the Magnuson Act let Chinese immigrants become citizens. And in 1952, another law extended this opportunity to all Asian immigrants and Asian Americans. They could now apply to become citizens. As citizens, they could register to vote.

▲ In 1965, thousands of protesters gathered throughout Alabama. Many faced arrest or violence.

In 1964, the Twenty-Fourth Amendment ended poll taxes. Still, other laws stood in the way of Black voters, especially in Southern states. Activists wanted to draw attention to these laws. In March 1965, they organized protest marches in Alabama. Their efforts gained national attention. As a result, Congress passed the Voting Rights Act in 1965. It ended the laws that kept Black people from voting. It also kept states from passing other limiting laws in the future. The act described how the US attorney general had to approve changes to voting laws. This person would make sure new laws didn't discriminate.

In 1975, the Voting Rights Act was expanded to protect language minorities. If more than 5 percent of citizens in an area spoke a language other than English, election information had to be in that language, too.

Voting rights also expanded to include younger people. In 1971, the Twenty-Sixth Amendment reduced the minimum voting age from 21 to 18. Activists began asking for this change during World War II (1939–1945) when the draft age was lowered to 18. If young people could be drafted, many Americans felt they should also be able to vote.

CASE STUDY

SNCC

Throughout the 1960s, many activists called for equal rights for Black Americans. The Student Nonviolent Coordinating Committee (SNCC) played a key role in this work. In addition to organizing protests, SNCC often focused on voting rights. SNCC believed voting was essential to improving the lives of Black Americans.

In 1964, Black Americans made up more than 40 percent of Mississippi's population. But only 7 percent of these Black Americans were registered to vote. SNCC worked to help more Black people register.

In some states, registering to vote was made purposely difficult. Each person had to fill out a form. This meant writing their name and address. People often had to explain part of the state constitution, too. So, SNCC members taught

▲ In 1964, SNCC helped organize the Freedom Summer project, which worked to register Black voters.

classes. They showed people how to read, write, and answer tricky test questions.

In several states, Black people faced violence if they tried to vote. Mobs gathered to scare them. Some Black voters were beaten or killed. Mobs also set people's homes on fire. This violence was meant to keep Black people from voting. Despite the danger, SNCC members kept working. They helped Black voters exercise their rights. SNCC also taught classes on nonviolent protest. People learned ways to stay calm and stand firm, even when facing hostile responses.

CHAPTER 3

HOW US ELECTIONS WORK

Voting is how US citizens choose their leaders. These leaders make laws and policies. Some leaders are part of local or state governments. Other leaders are part of the federal government. They make laws for the entire country. The federal government includes Congress and the president.

Members of Congress are elected by **popular vote**. Citizens choose which lawmakers represent their state. The US Senate has 100 members,

The US federal government, including Congress, is based in Washington, DC.

with two from each state. Senators serve six-year terms. The terms are staggered so one-third of senators are up for reelection every two years.

The US House of Representatives has 435 members. They are divided among the states based on population. Larger states have more representatives. For example, California has 52 seats in the House. Wyoming has just one.

Every 10 years, the US government takes a **census**. After this census, seats in the House are reassigned. Some states may lose seats if their populations have declined. Other states may gain representatives if their populations have increased. But the overall total stays the same.

Americans vote for the president, too. However, the president is chosen by the Electoral College. This is a group of 538 people called electors. Each state gets one elector for each member of Congress. Washington, DC, also gets three electors.

To become president, a candidate needs at least 270 electoral votes. In most states, the winner of the popular vote gets all the state's

Accurate for presidential elections in 2024 and 2028

19

electoral votes. Maine and Nebraska split their electoral votes based on who wins each **district**.

Supporters of the Electoral College say it keeps small states from being ignored. But candidates often focus on bigger states, especially swing states. Races in swing states are close, so winning them tends to have a bigger impact on the overall election. Critics say this is unfair.

Critics also say the Electoral College discourages voters. Individuals may feel that their votes don't matter. For example, Democratic candidates usually win the popular vote in Minnesota. That means they get all the state's electoral votes, even when elections are close.

> # THINK ABOUT IT
> **Do you think the Electoral College is a good way to select the US president? Why or why not?**

▲ In some states, candidates running for Congress spend more than $10 million on their campaigns.

Some voters also object to how the Senate is set up. All states elect just two senators. But some states have much bigger populations than others. As a result, a voter in a big state will have a much smaller impact on Senate elections.

Who pays for **campaigns** is another concern. Running for office costs millions of dollars. Often, rich people and big companies give money. Some voters worry that candidates could care more about these donors than about the people they're elected to represent.

CHAPTER 4

GERRYMANDERING

In presidential elections, votes are tallied up state by state. US Senate elections are similar. Each state's senators are decided by all the voters in that state. But in many other races, states are split up into smaller sections. These sections are called districts.

For example, most states have more than one member of the US House of Representatives. These states are divided into congressional

Voters in each district go to a different polling place to cast their votes.

districts. There is a separate district for each House seat. Voters in each district choose one representative for their area.

States are also divided into districts for **state legislature** races. For example, Texas has 31 state senators. Each one is elected by a different senatorial district. Texas is also split into 150 house districts. Voters in each district elect a state representative.

Like US House seats, state districts are adjusted after each US census. A government official looks at where people live in each state. Each state district should contain approximately the same number of people. If it does not, new borders are drawn for each district. Borders are also redrawn if a state loses or gains seats in the US House. The new borders divide the state's population evenly.

This is supposed to help each vote count equally. But sometimes new borders are designed to sway the results of elections. Doing this is called gerrymandering. It can happen in two different ways.

Cracking splits up groups of people who tend to vote the same way. For example, people in one part of a state may tend to elect Republican

CRACKING AND PACKING

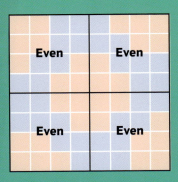

In some district shapes, voters from each party are about even.

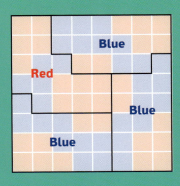

Cracking splits one party's members across several districts.

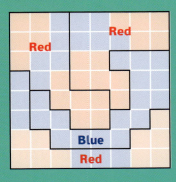

Packing can limit one party to winning a single district.

candidates. However, new borders can be drawn to split this area up. The area will now be part of several different districts. Republican voters form just a small part of each one. As a result, Republican candidates are less likely to win.

In contrast, packing groups similar people together. Most of the people who support one political party are put into one or two districts. The party's candidates will win there. But they'll likely lose in other districts. Lawmakers sometimes draw maps so an opposing party wins as few districts as possible.

In most states, a group of lawmakers from the state legislature makes the new districts. The party in power often draws maps to its own advantage. For example, Republicans dominated the 2010 election in Pennsylvania. Afterward, they redrew the state's US congressional districts.

▲ Many voters are concerned that gerrymandering is a new way of keeping certain people's votes from being counted.

Democratic votes were cracked. In 2012, most people in Pennsylvania voted for Democratic candidates. But because of the new borders, Democrats won only 5 of the state's 18 districts.

Gerrymandering can also affect state politics. In 2018, Wisconsin held an election for members of its State Assembly. Democrats won 53 percent of the votes. But because of gerrymandering, their party won only 36 percent of the seats.

CASE STUDY

RUCHO V. COMMON CAUSE

In 2016, a political group called Common Cause filed a lawsuit against the state of North Carolina. The North Carolina Democratic Party and several North Carolina voters also filed. Robert Rucho was named for the state. He was a Republican lawmaker. He'd led a group that made a new map of the state's congressional districts that year.

The lawsuit claimed this map was gerrymandered. It said the new districts gave Republicans unfair advantages. The lawsuit said this went against several parts of the US Constitution, including the First and Fourteenth Amendments. The lawsuit said the new borders were unfair to Black voters and kept some voters' voices from being heard.

▲ Common Cause has filed several lawsuits related to gerrymandering and voting rights.

In 2018, a court agreed and struck down the map. North Carolina appealed this ruling. Eventually, the case went to the US Supreme Court in 2019. After hearing the case, the Supreme Court dismissed it. It said gerrymandering was a political question, not a legal question. For this reason, the court did not have the power to change it.

Four justices disagreed with this ruling. They said the court had avoided an important issue. They felt it failed to protect the rights of voters.

CHAPTER 5

RESTRICTING VOTING

Most states limit voting rights for people convicted of **felonies**. In some states, people can vote after completing their prison sentences. In other states, people lose the right for the rest of their lives.

In some states, lawmakers wanted to add other restrictions and limits. In 2013, the Supreme Court made it easier for states to do this. The court ruled that Section 4 of the Voting Rights

In 2022, approximately 4.6 million people were unable to vote because of felony convictions.

▲ In 2022, 38 states asked voters to show some form of ID before casting ballots.

Act was **unconstitutional**. Section 4 explained which states had to get new voting laws approved. After the court struck this section, states added new restrictions. For example, Texas and Alabama began requiring voters to show IDs.

Supporters argue that ID laws prevent fraud. For example, they could stop people from voting under someone else's name. In many states, IDs must have a photo and be issued by the state. Many states will accept a driver's license. But not all adults have this form of ID. Critics point out that state IDs cost money. Often, people must visit a license office to get IDs. These offices can be hard for some people to reach. In 2015, for example, Alabama closed 31 license offices. Most were in majority-Black counties.

Investigations have found that voter fraud is extremely rare. Most claims of fraud turn out to be mistakes in recording information. However, fears about fraud remain. So do laws designed to stop it.

Some laws focus on same-day registration. This method lets people register at polling places on the day of the election. Opponents fear that people could register and vote at several different polling places. Computerized voting can help track if someone has already voted. But not all polling places have this. So, some states have ended same-day registration.

States may also limit third-party ballot returns. In this method, a voter completes a ballot and seals it in an envelope. Then someone else takes the sealed ballot to election officials. This method is helpful for people who live far from polling places or who have difficulty traveling. However, some states limit the number of ballots a person can collect. In Montana, for example, a person can bring in only six ballots. Other states don't permit this method at all. Officials claim this prevents fraud. Critics say these limits can keep some groups of people from voting, such as people who live in rural areas.

After the Supreme Court decision in 2013, several states also closed polling places. Some

▲ At some polling places, voters may have to stand in line for hours.

states wanted to cut costs. Others said having just a few central voting sites would be more efficient. However, these changes can make voting more difficult for some people. If a nearby polling place closes, voters must make longer journeys. Plus, larger polling places often have long lines. People who can't wait or don't want to may not vote.

CHAPTER 6

EXPANDING VOTING

Meanwhile, other lawmakers and activists want to help more people vote. This work starts with helping people register. For example, same-day registration can help new voters. Many states also offer online voter registration. People can submit a form on their computers or smartphones.

Some states use automatic registration. This often happens when someone gets or renews a

In 2016, Oregon became the first US state to begin automatic voter registration.

driver's license. The state's computer system also registers that person to vote. Some states do the same thing when people apply for government services, such as rental assistance or disability payments. People who don't want to register can opt out.

By 2022, 22 states were using some type of automatic registration. Supporters say people are more likely to vote if it's easier to do. Opponents say this isn't always helpful. If voting is too easy, people may not take it seriously enough.

Other work focuses on underrepresented voters. A group is underrepresented if not everyone who can vote does. For example, Latinos were 35 percent of California's adult population in 2019. But they were just 19 percent of the voters.

There are many reasons why people may not vote. Language is one of them. All US ballots

▲ The New York Voting Rights Act passed in 2022 and protected the voting rights of underrepresented groups.

are printed in English. The Voting Rights Act says some ballots must be printed in additional languages. These requirements are updated every five years. But only certain languages are included. Some, such as Arabic, are left out. To help, some cities print ballots in more languages than required. Activists are working to change the law. They want to include more languages.

▲ A drop box is a secure place where voters can turn in absentee ballots, which officials then collect and count.

Timing can be another barrier. Not everyone can make it to a polling place on Election Day. Absentee voting can help. This method lets people vote before Election Day. To do so, they may mail in their ballots or place them in drop boxes. In the past, people had to request absentee ballots in advance. And in some states, only certain groups of people qualified. In recent years, many states have expanded absentee voting. In Minnesota, for example, any voter can request an absentee ballot. And California mails ballots to all voters.

Several states have also expanded early voting. In Kentucky, for example, anyone can vote early. In-person voting is open a few days before an election. Often, only some polling places are open for early voting. But giving people more time to vote can help increase turnout.

Some activists also want to extend voting rights to people who have completed felony sentences. They say it's important for more people to have a say in government. But opponents say people who break the law must live with the consequences.

THINK ABOUT IT

Do you think states should restore voting rights to people with felony convictions? Why or why not?

CHAPTER 7

VOTER TURNOUT

Many Americans who could vote choose not to. During the 2020 presidential election, 158.4 million Americans voted. That was the highest voter turnout in decades. But it was only 63 percent of eligible voters.

Turnout for midterm and primary elections tends to be even lower. In primary elections, voters help choose their political party's candidate. Each party may start with several

Primaries and other smaller elections often have lower voter turnout. So do areas with more restrictions.

▲ By voting and supporting candidates, individuals can shape what their government looks like and does.

candidates. But only one goes on to the main election. Many people skip voting in primaries.

Midterm elections take place halfway through a president's term. Voters select senators and representatives. They also vote for state and local lawmakers. These smaller races often draw fewer voters. Only about half of eligible voters cast ballots in midterm elections in 2022.

Americans have many reasons for not voting. Some feel one vote is too small to make a difference. Others don't see candidates who share their views. There are several political parties in the United States. Yet only Democrats and Republicans have enough power to win major elections. Nearly half of people aged 18 to 49 said they wanted more choices.

Young adults often have low turnout. Their work or class schedules can be hard to predict. They may struggle to get to a polling place. Plus, young people often move to new places for work or school. This can make registration tricky.

People who are interested in politics are working to engage voters. They hold registration drives. They talk to people and post messages online. They encourage everyone to use their right to be heard.

THINK ABOUT IT

What can you do to encourage people you know to vote?

FOCUS ON
VOTING AND ELECTIONS

Write your answers on a separate piece of paper.

1. Write a paragraph explaining how voting rights in the United States have changed over time.

2. Do you think lawmakers should limit or expand early voting? Why?

3. Which part of Congress has an equal number of lawmakers for each state?
   - **A.** the Electoral College
   - **B.** the Senate
   - **C.** the House of Representatives

4. Why could California have a big impact on presidential elections?
   - **A.** It has 54 electoral votes, which is more than several other states combined.
   - **B.** It has more members of the US Senate than some other states.
   - **C.** It has a large population, and presidents are elected by popular vote.

Answer key on page 48.

GLOSSARY

amendment
A change or addition to a legal document.

campaigns
The activities and plans that people who are running for office use to try to get people to vote for them.

census
A count of an area's population.

district
One of several areas that a state is split into for an election.

felonies
Crimes that the government considers serious, often punishable by time in prison.

fraud
The crime of tricking others or using false information.

Indigenous
Native to a region, or belonging to ancestors who lived in a region before colonists arrived.

pandemic
A disease that spreads quickly around the world.

popular vote
Counting the total number of votes each candidate receives.

state legislature
The government body that makes laws and policies for one state.

unconstitutional
Not following the Constitution.

TO LEARN MORE

BOOKS

Jenkins, Tommy. *Drawing the Vote: The Illustrated Guide to the Importance of Voting in America*. New York: Abrams ComicArts, 2020.

Rubin, Susan Goldman. *Give Us the Vote! Over 200 Years of Fighting for the Ballot*. New York: Holiday House, 2020.

Rusch, Elizabeth. *You Call This Democracy? How to Fix Our Government and Deliver Power to the People*. Boston: Houghton Mifflin, 2020.

NOTE TO EDUCATORS

Visit **www.focusreaders.com** to find lesson plans, activities, links, and other resources related to this title.

INDEX

Congress, 12, 17–19
constitutional amendments, 10–13, 28

districts, 20, 23–27, 28

early voting, 5–6, 41
Electoral College, 18–20

gerrymandering, 25–27, 28–29

mail-in ballots, 6–7, 40
midterm elections, 43–44

polling places, 5, 33–35, 40–41, 45
poll taxes, 10, 12

presidential elections, 18–20, 23, 43
primary elections, 43–44

registration, 14, 33–34, 37–38, 45

Voting Rights Act, 12–13, 39

Answer Key: 1. Answers will vary; 2. Answers will vary; 3. B; 4. A